How I Lost
$1,500,000
In Missions

How I Lost
$1,500,000
In Missions

*(And What I Learned
from My Mistakes)*

John Addink

XULON PRESS

Xulon Press
2301 Lucien Way #415
Maitland, FL 32751
407.339.4217
www.xulonpress.com

Printed in the United States of America.

ISBN-13: 9781545657430

Praise for this book and author John Addink...

John Addink has written a must-read primer for anyone who desires to understand the principles of giving to overseas missions. Read this book and learn from John's wisdom.

-Randall Kennedy, Strategy Director,
The Maclellan Foundation, Inc.

I have come to appreciate John's application of his own business acumen to the complex challenge of reaching the world for Christ. This book tells that story. It is a very personal testimony that will encourage Great Commission Christians to become the best stewards they can be of the resources God has entrusted to them.
John has the courage to admit past mistakes, to challenge traditional assumptions, and to try fresh approaches.

-Dave Stravers, Author of *Measuring What Matters*

It is increasingly clear that changes in traditional mission strategies are required to meet the global changing environment we live in that now includes wide-ranging expulsion of NGOs from top mission fields around the world. John Addink's insight and wisdom in "How I Lost $1,500,000 in Missions" is a breath of fresh air that calls givers to seek long-term impact with their giving. Supporting key strategic groups like international student ministries-which have long-term *impact for advancing the Great Commission-provide Americans easy opportunities to reach people from otherwise unreached people groups who are already in America, living among us, and eager to meet and learn the American culture. John's book is filled with great new ideas for good stewardship in giving while reinforcing truths about the changing paradigms in missions. I strongly recommend John's book to every giver that wants to make a lasting impact for Christ!*

-**Doug Shaw,** President/CEO, International Students, Inc.

John Addink's experience as a businessman, innovator, and entrepreneur taught him a lot about investing in the right things; sometime applying costly lessons to correct his course. Lessons learned in business losses and gains are exceedingly valuable for missions giving too. Maybe mission donors have not always understood that, but John has and that has made the difference in his missions giving strategy. This book is timely reading for churches, mission agencies, and donors because God is using business experience and wisdom in twenty-first century mission giving like never before.

-**Gilles Gravelle, Ph.D.** Author of *The Age of Global Giving* and *A Guide for Donors and Funding Recipients of Our Time*

John Addink possesses the heart of a giver, the mind of a visionary and the experience of a successful leader. God has used this remarkable combination all over the world to bring others to Christ.

He has come alongside our ministry as well as many other ministries to support, encourage and challenge us to greater outcomes. Through 'How I Lost $1.5 in Missions', John offers a thought-provoking perspective on ministry and giving. This will challenge your thinking.

-**Josh McDowell,** www.josh.org

I pastored in denominational and nondenominational churches for over 40 years. I went on mission trips myself and also took dozens of people from my congregation to Asia, South America, and eastern Europe. My congregants were radically changed by going on mission trips. And, our giving to support American-sent missionaries and indigenous mission organizations increased significantly. However, John Addink's book has opened my mind to take seriously the great evangelistic impact that can happen when a significant investment is made in indigenous Christian leaders who are honest, integrous, and effective in evangelism. As a church leader and proponent of missions, you will be enriched and educated by John's thoughtful and proven principles for mission giving and stewardship.

-Dr. Larry Keefauver, Bestselling Author &
International Teacher

The successful spread of the gospel has resulted in extremely capable Christian leaders and workers all across the globe, a reality that raises hard questions about the proper role of Western human and financial resources in global missions. In this provocative book, Dr. John Addink has the courage to ask these hard questions, drawing on his decades of experience as a missions donor.

Although some will cringe at John's approach and conclusions, every one of us needs to wrestle with the issues he is raising. This is a very timely and helpful resource.

-Dr. Brian Fikkert. co-author of *When Helping Hurts: How to Alleviate Poverty Without Hurting the Poor...and Yourself*

Dedication

$\mathscr{I}$ dedicate this book to those who are interested in "making disciples" most effectively with what God has entrusted to them.

Acknowledgments

I thank my parents who have passed on, for teaching us "only what is done for Christ will last." I thank my wife Betty and Dr. Larry Keefauver for helping in putting this book on paper. I thank the many Americans who shared with me what they have learned in "making disciples." I thank the many nationals who did the work of "making disciples" that we could contribute to.

Table of Contents

Preface

What Does a Christian Businessman Know about Missions?

Knowledgeable people in the Christian publishing business tell us that authors need two traits to become trusted communicators in a book—experience and proven expertise over the years in their subject. Before I introduce you to my book's premise, permit me to share with you something of my experience and gained expertise.

I was born on a small farm in Iowa. My father immigrated from the Netherlands at twenty-one years old. Mother was also of Dutch ancestry.

There were nine children in our farming family. Our family was heartbroken when my younger brother Gerald passed away at eleven years old while playing with gas and fire in the cattails on the farm. Our faith in God and our knowledge that Gerald is now in heaven carry us through that difficult memory.

My parents believed in Christian education for all of us. Besides the cost of private education for all of us children, they were good contributors to the church and other Christian causes. The church published the members' yearly giving, and perhaps surprisingly, their giving exceeded even other families with fewer children and larger farms. This example from my faithful parents influenced our own giving early on. My wife and I tithed even during very lean times in our early years of married life.

My first introduction to foreign missions came from missionaries who visited our church as I grew up. The denominational publication that Mother made us read on Sundays also had articles on missions. During my college education in Agricultural Engineering, I even considered becoming an agricultural missionary. Perhaps it was particularly my mother who instilled in us that we should make a positive difference in the world.

My interest in foreign missions may also have been influenced by my love of travel, to see new places, and to meet and understand foreign people. I also interacted with many foreign students in my Agricultural Engineering education. After I started working in the field, I took trips to other countries as an irrigation consultant on short-term trips. As I advised them on effective irrigation methods, I enjoyed interacting with the local people and seeing how they lived.

I learned the risks of farming early on in life. Hail occurred for about 30 minutes on our Iowa farm. I did not think much of it until my father told me most of our crops were gone.

The personality God created me with has affected my last thirty years of giving. I had a strong desire to make money, and you could say that I'm competitive! My goal early on was to be wealthier than a church family that had a much larger farm than us. I was quite independent and dropped out of high school but went back the following year likely because I missed my fellow students.

My entrepreneurial nature and impulsiveness caused some challenges early in my life. I had three small business failures by age fourteen! One was raising rabbits. My mistake was that I built quite a few cages that housed too many rabbits before learning about the business. When I had enough feed in the rabbits that they should have weighed four pounds each, they only weighed two pounds. When I had failures, I usually quickly moved on in my life. I think my Mother prepared the rabbits left over for us to eat.

While going to a small local Christian school, our teacher for the four upper grades tried to get us to think outside the box. I built a crude contraption to invent perpetual motion. (It was not until I took engineering that I learned friction would make this impossible.) He taught us to think about new ways of doing things that had not yet been tried.

I met my wife on a blind date while at Calvin College in Grand Rapids, Michigan. She was also from a Dutch farming family of nine. They were poorer than us, and she earned her way through college. (I had earned part of my educational costs.) Betty and I have now been married for fifty-seven years and I am grateful for her friendship, love, and partnership throughout life.

Undaunted by early business mishaps, through the years I continued to start new businesses. I started a painting business in college. After graduation, I invested in rental housing. After graduating with my Master's Degree, I made irrigation sales on straight commission. After contracting highway irrigation, I manufactured irrigation equipment. Although it was also ultimately a failure, this experience led to a part-time university job and a Ph.D.

Despite or perhaps as a result of these early business experiences, along the way, I began to learn what it took to make a business successful. Because of my experiences early in life, my father was probably the most surprised when I started having business success!

I went on to establish sixteen sod farms in the western U.S. This has been my main for-profit business endeavor over the past forty-five plus years. We started very small with two other partners, one who was an excellent small farmer. My other partner was a good businessman and helped balance out my entrepreneurial nature. Together, we made solid business decisions. We grew a quality product and gave good service. We started with small farms and grew them gradually.

I was an entrepreneur and probably an adventurer before I learned to be a successful businessman. However, we have been blessed, and thus have been able to give millions to missions from profits in business.

Later, I began to apply the lessons I learned in business to mission decisions. I also worked to apply my capabilities to due diligence and focus. It is these lessons I have learned along the way, and the many, many souls who have come to trust in Christ and been discipled because of those lessons, that I wish to share with you.

Of course, one of our greatest joys in life is also our family. Betty and I have been married fifty-seven years, and we have been blessed with three children and eight grandchildren.

Now that you know a bit about my past experience and zeal for missions, let's turn to why as a Christian businessman I am writing about wise stewardship in missions.

-John Addink
California, 2018

Introduction

Realizing the Highest Return on Investment in Missions

What do I mean when I say I "lost" $1.5 million dollars in missions? I don't mean that the money was lost as we normally consider financial losses in business. However, considering "ROI" or *Return On Investment* is a business term that does fit my premise here. In business, prudent and successful ventures maximize a return on investment which also applies to wise stewardship. We desire the greatest return on the money invested in a joint venture.

The Church invests money in missions in order to receive the greatest return. By what do we measure the greatest ROI in missions? New disciples being made.

Our earlier investments in missions could have been done much more effectively. How that money was used did not maximize the return in saved persons. Here's my premise and how I will approach this issue of maximizing our investment in missions. Most of the $1.5 million "lost" could have been used in another approach to doing missions. Simply put, we would have reached many, many more people with the saving gospel of Jesus Christ with the funds we gave to missions. So perhaps it would be more appropriate to say that those *people* were "lost," at least in the sense that we were not able to reach them through the ineffective, costly methods we were using. Because of short-sighted stewardship decisions (and they are the same decisions and methods many, many people make today in missions), we lost the opportunity to share and disciple the gospel with thousands of people, many who had never heard the beautiful name of Jesus.

Our business success started taking off about 30 years ago. As our giving increased, we spent more time studying where it could be used more effectively. However, since our giving was increasing slowly and we were learning as we went, the lessons helped so the lost opportunity costs were not a great part of our overall life giving. As our giving increased from first tithing to more than 10%, then to 50%+ of our income and then to giving away part of our estate, we were giving to the national missions equivalent to medium to large megachurch mission budgets.

In addition to using ineffective methods, I also consider a loss occurring from not focusing early on, not doing effective due diligence, and being too entrepreneurial in mission programs. Being an entrepreneur in missions is not the problem but spending too much too early in mission entrepreneurial ventures is, before their effectiveness had been developed and established.

In my story, I will reveal how I made the biggest mistakes when we did not have much to give. As we learned, we quickly shifted mission giving to much higher impact areas, and by God's grace began to see more than a hundred thousand people come to Christ, become discipled, and helped through our support for missions. My prayer is that the Church and you, a believer motivated by the Great Commission, will learn from our mistakes!

This is not an idle inquiry! We have learned that, while Christians have made progress in reaching unreached people "groups," we are losing ground in world evangelization. Because the population growth of unreached peoples is exceeding our current efforts to reach them, we *must* explore and support more effective methods of reaching our world for Christ so that our return on investment is maximized for the glory of God!

We discovered that our greatest joy in missions giving happened when we started to network with and give funds to equip national Christian missionaries.

Investing in the equipping of national missionaries who could stay in their own country and who already knew the culture and the language was much more effective than the less effective missions support of sending Americans to do evangelization and discipleship among native peoples. Yes, we learned that while missions is not a business, we must use excellent business practices to maximize our assets in reaching the most "lost" people for Jesus Christ.

We learned this from several books and saw this confirmed on a trip years ago to the country in which we now focus our support for national missionaries. We then had the joy of seeing many, many more people reached, saved, and discipled. in the past twenty-five plus years than from our missions' support before that time. We have also had the great joy of meeting many, many fellow believers all over the world and making their ministry in Christ's name possible. Heaven rejoices over the salvation of the lost; our joy becomes greater and fuller when we invest our time, talent, and treasure in winning the lost through equipped, indigenous Christians!

Since then we have continued to focus our due diligence and efforts, do additional research, and spend time to help make many more disciples, particularly in one country where a great percentage of the unreached people of the world live.

Please read on. Regardless what you may think or have heard of the methods we believe are the most effective stewardship decisions to reach the world for Christ, I urge you to take the time to hear our story and consider how God may be calling you to apply it to your own missions' experience.

Chapter 1

Wise Stewardship and Opportunity Costs in Missions

I have some definitions to share with you:

> *Stewardship:* "The careful and responsible management of something entrusted to our care."

> *Opportunity Costs:* "The lost alternatives that cannot be pursued once another choice is made."

> *Stewardship in Missions:* "Applying wise stewardship and opportunity costs principles to missions giving and receiving."

An example of the principle of opportunity costs occurred on one of our southern California turf farms this past year. We were short on St. Augustine grass inventory and looking at the options for the remaining five acres of inventory ready to sell. We knew we could:

(1) sell it and buy sprigs to replant acres we needed, or
(2) keep it and turn it into sprigs to replant needed acres.

From these two alternatives, we quickly determined that the maximum return from the five acres was to use it for replanting rather than sell it and then ship in new sprigs from out of state.

However additional research yielded an even better, third alternative. Since St. Augustine had been a minor product for us until then, we had never studied how large growers brought back their St. Augustine inventory after harvest. In doing so, we learned that the usual practice was to leave a ribbon of grass to grow in for the next harvest. Additional research by our general manager revealed that plugging our five acres from the remaining turf would go much further than sprigging for replanting. A plugging machine would need to be purchased, but we would get much more for the sod we sold from the five acres that would not be required for replanting if we plugged rather than planted sprigs.

In the end, our cost savings was $50,000 or more. To make a wise decision, it required thinking about more options to do the desired job and avoiding the opportunity costs that would be lost if an unwise decision was chosen.

How does the principle of opportunity cost apply in missions? We look at church planting and other missions giving as a call to wise stewardship of resources and efforts, with eternal returns or harvests continuing long into the future. The implications for opportunity costs could not be more far-reaching. Our great call to make disciples requires the highest level of our talents, research, analysis, effort, and thought.

This book examines the opportunities that are lost when we spend our mission's efforts and resources on ineffective methods. Sending missionaries who reach fewer people at a much higher cost without analyzing the relative effectiveness of mission's work, instead of making disciples by supporting known, faithful national missionaries, with much lower cost per missionary, is much less effective in reaching lost people with the saving message of Jesus' love.

This book presents what we have learned over the past thirty years based on solid evidence and research. Yes, there is a cost up front in doing the due diligence to research the options which may involve sending someone on the field.

In response to our call to wise stewardship and due analysis of effectiveness in missions, some may say that God is ultimately responsible for salvation and for the response of any person or peoples to His gospel. I agree 110 percent. Without God's Spirit and blessing, nothing can be done, and nothing that is done can be done without Him. In fact, this principle holds true throughout life—He is sovereign in all things and directs our paths and results. However, this fact does not relieve us of our responsibility to be wise stewards of the gifts, talents, and resources He has given us, or excuse us for making poor choices and working ineffectively.

In the Parable of the Talents, Christ makes a strong call for "faithfulness" over the resources our heavenly Father entrusts to us. Surely this parable applies above all to the resources He has given us to yield a "harvest" unto eternity. We are responsible to Him to work excellently unto Him. Our compassion for the lost of this world compels us to seek to reach them with the most effective and far-reaching methods available. I believe that God's command to be wise stewards does not end at the missions' frontier.

In *Helping Without Hurting in Short Term Missions*, authors Steve Corbett and Brian Fikkert discuss opportunity costs: "For every investment of our resources, whether time, money, or energy, there is something else we could have done with those resources instead."[1] For example, if one has a thousand dollars or a hundred thousand to give, once it is given for one cause, it is not available to give to another cause. The concepts of opportunity costs can apply to mission giving.[2]

For example, in *Helping Without Hurting in Short Term Missions*, the cost of short-term missions is estimated to be *between*

---

[1] Corbett, Steve & Fikkert. Brian. *Helping Without Hurting in Short Term Missions, 2014*. Illinois: Moody Publishing. p. 32

[2] Corbett, Steve & Fikkert. Brian. *Helping Without Hurting in Short Term Missions, 2014*. Illinois: Moody Publishing. p. 32

$1.6 billion and $2.2 billion a year. The authors state that the problem is not that so much money is being spent for short-term missions, but "how inefficiently the money is used when allocated to traditional STMs (short term missions)."[3]

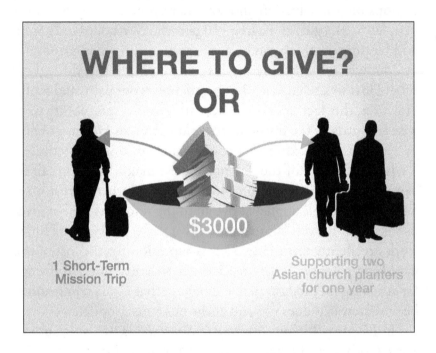

Opportunity Cost. Once the money is used for a short-term American mission trip, it is not available to help national missionaries serve in more effective ways. Other possibilities for $3,000 include Children's Bible Clubs offered by indigenous churches for 2000 children for 10 days, or Christian literacy and arithmetic training taught by local Christians for 100 adults for one year!

---

[3] Corbett, Steve & Fikkert. Brian. *Helping Without Hurting in Short Term Missions, 2014.* Illinois: Moody Publishing, p. 32

Corbett and Fikkert go on to discuss the salary of local church planters: $1440 to $4320 a year in Asia while American church planters may cost $36,000 to $72,000 a year.[4]

An American missionary overseas has to struggle to be effective compared to a Christian national. On top of all of this, the cost of funding an American missionary is exponentially higher than training and equipping the local Christian.

In *Measuring What Matters*, Dave Stravers, an American who has served full time in overseas mission work, discusses how the world for missions started changing about forty years ago. "Two centuries of Great Commission activity had successfully implanted the Gospel in almost every geo-political nation. A new paradigm was born--one that encouraged Western Christians to send or support "native missionaries" as opposed to Western missionaries."[5]

Another missionary leader stated that, "the best workers to recruit are people from the country where the (unreached) people

4   Corbett, Steve & Fikkert. Brian. *Helping Without Hurting in Short Term Missions, 2014.* Illinois: Moody Publishing. p. 32

5   Stravers, Dave. *Measuring What Matters.* 2012. Michigan. Mission India.

group lives." Often the nationals know the culture and language, making them much more effective at a much lower cost than what it takes for an American to travel to the country, learn the language, and try to work in a foreign culture.

In "Indian Sending," from *Perspectives*, K. Rajendran, an Indian author discusses how from 1947 when Western mission agencies began to withdraw through the 1960s as new indigenous Indian missions emerged, India missions went from needing training, to being able to train their own people, and then to the "largest missions association in the world with more than 220 organizations sending out nearly 50,000 Indian workers" in India.[6] We believe these indigenous missions organizations should also be considered by Christians who wisely seek to be good stewards in their missions giving.

Based on my experience, my application of opportunity costs in missions leads to the following steps:

1. Determine the goal or objective to achieve in giving.
2. Identify the various options or opportunities that could achieve the goal or objective.
3. Estimate the cost and potential returns from the main options available. This requires evaluation and study.
4. Support the selected missions group or missionary.
5. Follow-up on the gift(s) given to try to determine what results were obtained and make adjustments as needed.

The process is then repeated, and new options may be included to consider. Usually for best results, long-term investments, follow-up inspections, and continued knowledge acquisition are required.

Our past thirty years of learning and continued mission giving can be broken up into the above five steps with some explanations.

---

[6] Rajendran, K. Page 373. "Majority World Sending." *Perspectives. US Center for World Missions.* 2009. California. William Carey Library.

These principles can be applied to the decision where to direct missions efforts. About six years ago, I decided we should focus on one southeast Asian country that is one of the most unreached countries in the world. We had been involved there for twenty-five years. There are many unreached people groups who have never heard the gospel, with followup to make disciples. The people we serve were put down by their religion, and their hearts were open to the knowledge that Jesus gives them hope here on earth and for eternity. The cost to equip national Christians to spread the gospel was very low. Only 2-4 percent of the country may be Christians. While this still works out to many, many indigenous Christians, it leaves a tremendous number of non-Christians, many who had never heard the gospel. Given the greatly increased effectiveness of indigenous missionaries, these were considered the best use of our resources to help reach the country with the good news of God's love for them.

Many opportunities presented themselves as worthy receipts of donations. These included television, radio, and tools to help indigenous churches and mission's organizations. Because they know their own people and culture, we study and select faithful, effective organizations to support, and then let them pick their own tools. We continue to follow them and ask questions as needed.

A big question that arises is how to be accepted in an unreached people group. By following Christ's call to help those in need, one could drill wells or even start large social help programs. We have seen very low-cost programs such as Christian-taught holistic adult literacy and children's clubs, with their social benefits and opportunities to learn about Christ, provide wonderful opportunities to demonstrate Christ's love for all people.

I have seen several mission leaders advise American Christians to go themselves if they know of an Unreached People Group (UPG) or an Unengaged Unreached People Group (UUPG). Many times the advice is to find the "man of peace." How someone without experience in a country and not knowing the language or the culture applies this concept, at least in the early years, is confusing to me. It could take many years to begin to understand the language and make any inroads into a foreign culture. I have followed up on two churches' efforts to reach UUPGs by sending Americans. While they were sending Americans short and long term to a UUPG, I studied and identified local national mission organizations I trusted to send indigenous church planters from nearby to go to the same place to proclaim the gospel with the support we gave. The results and striking comparisons from one of these examples is given in a later chapter, "Why We Support Nationals." The church spent $200,000 over two years to learn what the national mission organizations already knew.

Usually what I have observed is that a church would send a number of their congregation to the UUPG. Besides the costs for foreigners, often with no experience, trying to figure out what to do, the presence of many Americans made it look like a foreign religion. Our children and grandchildren went to view a mission project they supported. My son-in-law still tells of how they disrupted a project they were supporting with too many white Americans and had to quickly leave. In many countries, the presence of many Westerners only hinders the work instead of making it more effective.

Some may say, despite the existence of a local church and ministries in the areas surrounding the area they wish to reach, that they prefer to send one or two long-term American missionaries and allow them to head up an organization that is otherwise staffed by indigenous people. In addition to the exponentially higher cost for this method of outreach, the studies also show that this is not what American-sending missionaries will do. One would hope that they would train trusted people in the area, who would begin to multiply the efforts to reach the surrounding area. "And the things you have heard me say in the presence of many witnesses entrust to reliable people who will also be qualified to teach others" (2 Timothy 2:2).

A study comparing native church planters and Americans shows that the average American church-planting organization actually spent very little time training and entrusting the gospel to indigenous leaders, and the western people continue to do a great deal of the work themselves. See Missionary Cost Effectiveness Summary in a later chapter.

As a result, instead of the exponential growth that one can see from the work of low-cost indigenous workers, the Americans continue to slowly add new believers and churches. It's not that good isn't being done, but the relatively ineffective methods and the failure to entrust the gospel to multiplication through trustworthy Christians in the reached country indicates that this is poor stewardship at best. In addition to showing a disregard for the faithful work of the generations of missionaries who have served in the past, the many of believers who have already come to Christ all over the globe, and the beauty of the local church around the world, this attitude also ignores the tremendous impact that can occur when God's trustworthy people and his Church within a country are equipped and empowered to reach their own people for Christ.

I discussed American-led missions with an economics professor. He said American companies learned many years ago to have foreign branches led by nationals from the country in which the business was located. One would hope, since Christianity is an eastern religion that came westward, that we would be prepared to entrust the beautiful gospel message to indigenous peoples who actually live nearer to the areas to which the gospel originally spread, and who are eager to reach the nearby peoples for Christ.

In order to assess the effectiveness of mission's work and various methods, it is essential to receive and monitor results, and to compare them with other available missions methods. I look back on some early foreign missions work we supported and wondered why there was no **due diligence** done on effectiveness of ministry and impact before large sums were expended. When I ultimately did the research on the effect of the mission's work, the organization likely would not have been happy with what I found.

**Do your due diligence on missions' expenditures
and determine the eternal harvest in souls on what you
are doing and how you can have better
stewardship and results.**

In our own personal mission's support, we ended up focusing on five indigenous church planting groups in one of the most unreached countries in our world. Because it is important to continue to assess the effectiveness of the work being supported, we continue to spend some money on short-term trips to evaluate these national ministries. **We believe some short-term trips are advised and essential.** In order to monitor results, in proportion to our level of support, we supported an evaluator for four years, including two five- to six-week trips a year. We continue to do cross checking with others who have knowledge of the missions we support or are considering supporting, including our recent inspection trip. We seek to keep these total costs down to 5 percent of the total support being sent to a particular area.

Another example of opportunity costs is the one million international students and many immigrants in America, many who remain unreached while here in our own country. We work with local outreach groups to introduce them to Christianity and disciple them. While it may be difficult for us as Americans to reach someone living in another country, we can easily follow up with foreign students studying in our local community, which is not true of most so called "short-term mission trips." Sadly, most of the international students never even enter the home of an American. We also support a ministry to reach immigrants and refugees who are living in our community. These people are already here, among us, and often eager to meet Americans and learn about our culture. When they do trust in Christ, members from both of these groups bring the gospel back to their own countries.

We have observed the sad fact that while Americans are busy sending people to other countries, where their effectiveness is questionable and where little to no follow-up can occur, we are almost completely neglecting the ripe local mission opportunities where we could be effective, to reach foreign peoples who live in our own neighborhoods and towns.

Charity Giving Season states that, "75 percent of all donors don't do any research."[7] before making a donation. Another source says that 50 percent of business people, who have the tools to apply principles of good stewardship to their giving, do not do any research before giving. Most missions giving is based on good stories. Any mission person has a few good stories to tell. Stories are not outcomes but rather motivators. Stories are poor indicators for effective missions giving.

While reading about a Peace Corp worker in Paraguay living on $100 a month maybe 15 years ago, I wondered if I would believe in supporting an American in a UPG if he or she was willing to live on the same salary as is earned by those receiving ministry. But besides the living costs, the extra cost is still in learning the language and culture, which can take years, and furloughs. Perhaps ironically, the Peace Corps worker I read of learned to know God through a native Paraguayan he was working with.

My brother worked in missions in the Caribbean for some years. He tells of two American missionaries, who would not allow the nationals with whom they were sharing the gospel to enter their home. We have seen other American missionaries living in a compound separate from the people they are trying to reach with the gospel. These stories only serve to illustrate what we already know about the high cost of sending American missionaries, who are unfamiliar with the local culture and do not know the language.

Another challenge with supporting an American without going beyond stories is accountability. It is difficult to measure the impact of an isolated individual missionary sent to another country. We prefer to provide for a national indigenous missionary, working under the umbrella of an indigenous national organization that is known to keep their own local missionaries

---

[7] "Giving Season." *The Press-Enterprise News*, (12/18/15) p.3.

accountable. Accountability for an American who raises his or her own funds may be difficult in the US. Unconnected from the local church in another country, it is much more difficult to keep an American accountable in either short or long-term overseas work.

"Opportunity cost analysis" can also be used to decide in which countries we will seek to support missions work. Several years ago, we decided to concentrate our efforts on one southeast Asian country in one of the most unreached areas of our world. As Paul once said, "I make it my ambition to preach the gospel, not where Christ has already been named, lest I build on someone else's foundation, but as it is written, 'Those who have never been told of Him will see, and those who have never heard will understand'" (Romans 15:20-21). Even in these unreached areas, there are nearby trustworthy Christians and churches, eager to reach their country for Christ. All they may lack are the resources to go, and this is what we seek to provide.

As we assess the effectiveness of a missions effort, we believe the most important objective is making disciples of Christ, and secondly, the physical well-being of the people being reached. Physical needs are important and mentioned often in the Bible. Indeed, the Kingdom of Heaven on earth is not only spiritual, but also physical.

When He first began His ministry, Christ went to the synagogue and read from Isaiah, "The Spirit of the Lord is upon me, because He has anointed me to proclaim good news to the poor. He has sent me to proclaim liberty to the captives and recovering of sight to the blind, to set at liberty those who are oppressed, to proclaim the year of the Lord's favor." As our Lord sat down, He said (referring to Himself), "Today this Scripture has been fulfilled in your hearing" (Luke 4:18-21).

We do also see a positive spiral resulting from spiritual new life in Christ: once people start becoming disciples, and their hearts begin to change, the money spent for alcohol and gambling is used for their own betterment. As a church develops, the members start helping each other including taking in widows, orphans and the sick.

Take These Essential Steps...

After each step, write out a paragraph action plan about what you and/or your church plan to do for effective due diligence:

1. Determine the goal or objective to achieve in giving.
2. Identify the various options or opportunities that could achieve the goal or objective.
3. Estimate the cost and potential returns from the main options available. This requires evaluation and study.
4. Support the selected missions group.
5. Follow-up on the gift(s) given to try to determine what results were obtained and make adjustments as needed.

Chapter 2

Applying Lessons from Business and Professional Life

How can we most effectively reach and disciple the world for Christ faithfully using the gifts, talents, and resources with which we have been entrusted?

As turf farmers, we attempt to be a low-cost producer of quality sod. This basic axiom, applied in many ways throughout our business, has stood us in good stead for five decades. I now carry this thought over into overseas evangelism and discipleship programs, applying lessons from business and professional life.

> One of my lessons in business was to **focus on the primary goal.**
> Another important one was to only go into a new venture slowly while doing **due diligence.**
> (With my entrepreneurial spirit, these were both hard for me to do at times!)

I also learned in my profession as an irrigation engineer, there are **many variables**, and it's not always easy to define what causes what.
(With sixteen different sod farms across the country, most of my many managers did not want to be judged based on what another manager did in another market, climate, and soil type.)

Standard Measures of Comparison

Business: In our sod farming operations, we rely on standard measures of comparison among all our farms. This includes labor costs, fertilizer, seed, and irrigation costs. This helps us to show a farm manager where his costs might be too high. Then we look at variables such as pumping depth to allow for differences for each farm, but do not give much allowance for variables such as labor.

As we continued to hone and adjust our metrics as needed, we were able to make decisions based on our best knowledge as we continued to learn from fifty years of experience. Because we had more than one farm from which to make comparisons, we were able to determine over time how different factors affected our harvests and our results.

Mission Support: I also seek to assess the work methods and results in mission support giving to several church planting groups. Deciding on funding among various national missions through evaluation and inspecting results is not easy. One can start out with giving the majority to mainly fund individual Americans on short-term or long term-trips. This is the road most easily traveled, but likely not the best one to take in the long-run. The effectiveness is much lower, and the rewards are likely much less than taking the effort to engage and give to equip national mission groups. Fortunately, this is also a path that has already been traveled by some and can be followed by many others as well.

The results in business were much easier to measure than foreign mission's work.

Financial Assessments: The financial statements were a good measure. These were not exact since the inventory, maturity, and quality were not exact numbers. In business, during the initial or startup years a farm had losses or investment costs. We learned that it would usually take a year or two to tell if a new manager was capable of being successful.

In missions, it is essential to assess how the funds are being used, as well as who is being reached and discipled. To do this, we try to determine if the national missions we support are multiplying churches based on making disciples. Making assessment even more difficult, results given by some American and national mission groups can at times be viewed with a degree of skepticism.

After due diligence, I found I am less concerned about the $2,000 that may have been wasted on a national pastor than the $70,000 per year on an American who does not know the language nor the culture and does not always have reasonable supervision. There are stories of loss and failure in both groups, but the *benefits* of entrusting the gospel to indigenous missionaries, and the *costs* of an American missionary gone awry, are both significantly greater.

Environmental Influence: In my study of individual methods and outcomes in missions, it quickly became obvious that results are quite different depending on one's environment. For example, On the Open Door's World Watch List, India is #15 among all nations in persecution and hostility toward the gospel with a score of 73. Saudi Arabia is #14, just above India, with a score of 76.[8] This is also true between different parts of the same country with church planting results. It can take time before the first convert comes about in a new region.

Impact and Effectiveness of Workers: We agree that measuring impact and effectiveness of various workers and ministries

---

[8] Opendoorsusa.org

in missions can be difficult. However, one has to be cautious within a country and similar environment when one church planter has many fewer converts compared to another. For example, I hear that results among comparable Bible translators may vary by five to one. Studies of self-supported US mission workers shows that the amount of time spent in ministry may vary up to 50 percent. In other words, some work twice as hard as others, which affects the outcome of their work.

Impacts in the same area and Unreached People Group (UPG) among ministries and missionaries can vary considerably. My own observations on hiring and observing worker results caused me to conclude many people are better off working under a good manager who will provide more accountability and improve their results.

We do not support many self-supported individual mission workers since my observation is that usually they are mostly on their own in managing their time and results. Their support is not dependent on their organization, but on the stories and results they report to their donors. I have seen this both in the US and with American missionaries overseas.

Having an entrepreneurial personality can cause problems in business as well as in missions' giving.

Business: As our business improved, I sometimes would rush into other ventures **without** due diligence and with little knowledge. I had a few tough lessons before I decided due diligence was essential for any new business venture. I think the lesson is to start small and expand as success comes, but with due diligence in all facets of any new venture.

Missions: Over time, I realized more and more that we must be willing to do due diligence with our missions' funding as well. We need to do due diligence so that we are giving wisely to ministries that actually work effectively to accomplish the objectives and purposes for which they were established. It is just plain and simple wise stewardship to ask questions and follow up with those to whom we've given funds. We need to continually ensure we are doing all we can to carefully use the resources and talents with which we've been entrusted.

Focus on Discipleship

Of course, this begins with questions about what we are ultimately about. I believe that means our focus is to make disciples and teach them everything that Christ has taught us. Our own giving journey has caused us to consider various methods of evangelism and the importance of focusing on effective methods of teaching and discipling those new believers.

Counting raised hands at an invitation indicates little about making disciples (Matthew 28:19) unless there is good follow-up. Counting baptisms is more meaningful, but perhaps less meaningful than counting disciples that are measured by Bible study, prayer time, church attendance and witnessing. Another way may be to count churches and their average attendance. *Measuring What Matters* is also the title of a book by David Stravers.

When I was an extension irrigation engineer, I heard a story of a county agent who received an award for his achievements. When asked what made him so successful, he said, "I see which way the crowd is going and then run in front of it with the flag." Unfortunately, sometimes I see this same concept as American missionaries take credit for God's blessing on the work of national missionaries.

There is also a natural tendency to justify the effectiveness of our own methods despite evidence to the contrary. By asking questions and analyzing supporting information, I have learned that many results are inflated. For example, a short-term missions trip to claim many decisions for Christ is always questionable. I say this because discipleship requires time for making disciples, usually much more than the two weeks or less generally allotted to a short-term mission trip. David Platt's book "Radical,"[9] discusses the quick so-called conversions compared with the time required in the discipling process which I recommend to you for reading.

We have seen this in working with international students who have become Christians. As the Holy Spirit works in a person's heart, conversions and making disciples takes time. Although there are examples in the Bible of the 3,000 and 5,000 converting at one time, my own experience and that of David Platt show we would be wise to at least question quick results. Furthermore, Christ calls us to follow up with teaching and discipling, so new believers are added to the numbers of a local church body. This also helps planting new churches in UPGs.

We have learned that sometimes people will raise their hands to please their guests, to get the gifts presented, or to add to the many gods they already believe in. Some converts are counted two or more times by whoever may give them biblical teaching. It is

---

[9] Platt, David. *Radical* Multnomah Books 2010

only over a sustained period of time that we can be sure they have understood and are growing in their faith.

We did a Jesus Film distribution to our city. A study was made of decisions to accept Christ as Savior resulting from the distribution. When a question was asked if this was the first time a decision was made half said it was not. We also did not see the physical evidence in the churches of new decisions.

I reviewed reports recently of indicated decisions counted versus new churches planted and compared it to new disciples or new believers counted versus new churches planted. My conclusion was that as few as 5% of indicated decisions may end up as new disciples or believers. It depends on the follow up and discipleship is the best way for me to explain this. A business can base decisions on gross sales or net profits. Usually net profits determine the health and growth of a business.

In business, we have a saying that what gets measured, gets managed. Since it takes disciples or believers to have a multiplying church in a UPG, we look for new believers and new churches planted counted, how they are counted and some auditing of results, so we have some assurance of lasting results. We also look at whether the numbers are believable.

In business, I quickly learned that God created each of us differently. I went to several seminars on understanding different personality traits to help make sure I hired and led well. For a manager, we needed someone who wanted to do activities in a very timely manner and did not procrastinate. Furthermore, once we knew what was required for a successful sod farm, we did not want a manager who constantly wanted to innovate and do things in new and different ways. Although we always value thoughtful leadership, the manager's job is to send out consistently good quality product on a timely basis every day.

My personality as a creative entrepreneur would make me a bad fit as a farm manger. My gifts are for big picture thinking and creating a successful path for others to follow and implement each day. In effect, I am discipling managers. Together, we built a team that functions successfully to grow strong, beautiful turf, and then deliver and install it to the customer's needs and specifications.

For someone in the business office, a more structured personality is required to accurately keep the numbers. For the field workers, we need someone who is teachable and will respond to the oversight of the foreman. With truck drivers, we do a test drive. Many drivers who said they had ten years of experience seem to have had just one year of experience ten times over, rather than building ten years of experience!

In missions, my question becomes, who evaluates short and long-term missionaries to determine whether they are well suited to mission's work? I have heard it said that to be successful in evangelizing abroad, one must first be successful in one's own home country. A wise couple I know asks potential missionaries to serve with international students in their home town for a year before giving them funds for short-term missions abroad.

I wonder if this may also be the case for short-term missionaries repeating trips to various countries. Are many like the truckers who, rather than driving like they have ten years of experience, seem to repeat the same novice experiences over and over without becoming seasoned in sharing their faith with others in the country where they go?

I have met many Americans who have made tremendous sacrifices to go to the field to minister, and they do accomplish good. We cannot criticize their willingness to sacrifice and go. However, we also need to recognize that it can seem much more exciting and virtuous to be a missionary rather than to stay in the US and do evangelical work with international students and immigrants. When they do go, many American missionaries seem to have a hard time understanding how to apply the scriptural guidance to entrust the gospel and train a few faithful workers who will teach others in their country. If they did understand the concept of supporting nationals to win souls for Christ, they could raise or donate funds for them rather than going overseas themselves. What they give would produce far more fruit than what they would likely experience from going themselves.

Likewise, we must be certain that we are carefully evaluating the national indigenous organizations that we support. I have run across a national leader who had not been trained in good management but had fifty people answering directly to him. This would not work well in a church or organization here in the U.S. and was most likely not effective management and oversight in that country either.

If the need is for us to equip and support,
what is the next best use of our resources, gifts, and talents?

We believe that our resources, gifts, and talents are often badly misallocated. We are using our resources to go where we are only minimally effective instead of using those resources to equip those who could effectively reach their own countries. At the same time, we are failing to reach the lost in our own neighborhoods and cities because we have placed our focus elsewhere. We have overlooked and ignored those we could effectively reach here in our local mission field.

Sadly, we are ignoring our responsibility toward the huge mission field in our own country that is crying out for workers. The unreached missions field for Americans is the 1,000,000 foreign students who come here for a short while. Many are from countries hostile to allowing missionaries to come and share the gospel. Most of them are never presented the gospel nor get into a Christian home. The other large U.S. mission field is among the immigrants and refugees who come here bringing other beliefs.

What have we learned from other people to move toward better stewardship of our resources and opportunities? Are we willing to put what we have learned into practice?

Take These Essential Steps...

After each step, write out a paragraph action plan about what you and/or your church plans to do to move toward better stewardship of your resources and opportunities by applying lessons learned from effective business and professional practices.

- Focus on the primary goal—discipleship.
- Go into a new venture slowly while doing due diligence.
- Seek to assess the work methods and results in your mission support giving.
- Check financial statements to assess how the funds are being used, as well as who is being reached and discipled.
- Attend seminars on understanding different personality traits or find a volunteer familiar with personality traits.
- Ask who evaluates short or long-term missionaries to determine whether they are well suited to mission's work.
- Interact with international students for a year in your own home town.

Investigate the large U.S. mission field among the immigrants and refugees who come here bringing other beliefs.

Chapter 3

Learning from Others

*W*e have learned so much from others. We are grateful that they have taken the time to write books, share with us in person, and help us learn about effectiveness in world missions.

I started out learning to tithe from my parents supporting American missionaries. After supporting Jesus Film and then taking a trip to India to negotiate coating of the film, we met strong CRU Indian Christians who did evangelism, discipleship, and training with occasional financial and business help for much less money than American missionaries required.

Being a reader and a researcher (Ph.D.) I started looking for more information on the subject. I came up with many arguments by other Christians that supported what we had found out and continued to learn including more trips to learn about supporting other nationals.

We read Bob Findley's book, "The Future of Foreign Missions"[10] which provides good evidence for equipping nationals rather than sending Americans. Bob left China many years ago after asking the Christian Chinese what he could do to help them. They said, "The best thing American missionaries could do for the spread of

---

[10] Finley, Bob. *The Future of Foreign Missions*. 2003. Virginia. Christian Aid Mission

the gospel in China was to go home. They were making it appear as a bourgeois religion." He then started spreading the word and raising support to help equip national Christians. It is amazing how the gospel spread in China after the American missionaries were expelled. Appearance of many American Christians in other countries also can make Christianity appear to be a foreign religion, when in fact it is a middle-eastern religion that only relatively recently moved westward.

Promising changes have been occurring in Bible translation as well. The Seed Company, an affiliate of Wycliffe Bible Translators, translates the gospel through nationals and a few Americans, to those who have not heard, with 85 percent less cost and 60 percent less time. What might have taken old Bible translation methods many decades to allow a people group to read the Bible in their own language, can now take only a few years. As a result, many more are reached much sooner with the saving knowledge of Jesus Christ!

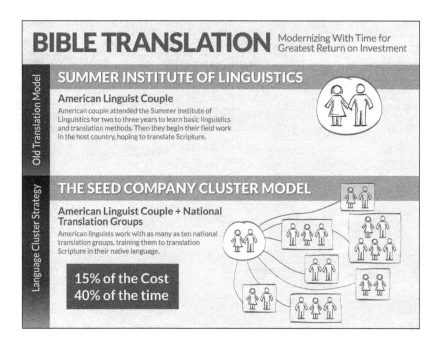

BIBLE TRANSLATION — Modernizing With Time for Greatest Return on Investment

Old Translation Model

SUMMER INSTITUTE OF LINGUISTICS

American Linguist Couple

American couple attended the Summer Institute of Linguistics for two to three years to learn basic linguistics and translation methods. Then they begin their field work in the host country, hoping to translate Scripture.

Language Cluster Strategy

THE SEED COMPANY CLUSTER MODEL

American Linguist Couple + National Translation Groups

American linguists work with as many as ten national translation groups, training them to translation Scripture in their native language.

15% of the Cost
40% of the time

Wycliffe started Bible translation many years ago with the first model shown above, the Summer Institute of Linguistics. About twenty-five years ago, The Seed Company was started. It is an offshoot of Wycliffe, but still associated with it. Translation costs can be about 85 percent less and are completed in 60 percent less time. It uses a cluster model with SIL and national personnel in partnership. The new cloud sourcing or Crowd Seed shows promise to increase the speed, accuracy, and decrease the costs of translation even further. We can learn much from this example for world missions.

We also learned that many of the reasons westerners use for sending Americans are not actually supported by facts. For example, many western churches say that those who go on short-term mission trips grow in their faith and develop a stronger affinity to support foreign missions. But some studies do not support this belief.

"Lessons from The Sapling" by Kurt Alan Ver Beek,[11] and the study of others, show almost no long-term effects in the lives of most short-term mission's participants (See the Figure below). Not only did the funds spent to send them yield questionable results in the visited country with little measurable long-term results in their own spiritual lives, they did not have extra funds available to give for a national project after going since they often raised money from others to go on the trip. Ver Beek showed that their own giving to missions usually did not increase after going either.

---

[11] Ver Beek, Kurt Alan. 2007. *Lessons from the Sapling: Review of Quantitative Research on Short Term Missions*. kverbeek@calvinedu.

Many Christians believe that short-term mission trips have a great effect on the participants. "Lessons from the Sapling" by Ver Beek, and the study of others, show almost no long-term effects on most participants.

We have seen that very few who go on short-term mission trips work with international students or immigrants living here in the U.S. before or after going. It is as though their mindset is that mission work is "over there" and only they are capable of doing it. Gary Chapman in Home Life Team, SBC, states, "We are in a position to teach our children that we can be missionaries without going to another country."[12]

Barna Research Group shows, "People who took *domestic* service trips reported the same degree of life-changing experiences as did those traveling abroad."[13]

Jim Haaries questions short-term effectiveness and raises the possibility of longer-term damage caused by the westerners' lack of cultural sensitivity. For example, using high-cost, glossy American

---

[12] Chapman, Gary. *"Missions at Home."* Homelife. November 2008. SBC. p. 5

[13] Barna Group. August. 2008.

materials for a short-term Vacation Bible School in a poor foreign country has messed up the indigenous students' future desires to attend VBS hosted by a local church with simple, locally-produced materials.[14]

We have met those who paid for their own trip, rather than raising support from others, and have extra money later to give to the national missions they visited, and they continued to follow up. This type of exploratory "vision" trip may be a more effective reason for short-term travels or missions.

Unfortunately, from my own conversations with many of those who have gone on short-term trips, I have not received confirmation that they then understand that most evangelism and discipleship is actually done by the nationals they may have visited and not the Americans overseas long term.

It would be nice if we could at least say that our lack of effectiveness in missions individually is harmless, because any slack is taken up by the sheer number of westerners who go and share the gospel on foreign mission fields. Unfortunately, trusted experts in the field say *we are losing ground in world evangelism. Operation World's State of the World Plenary 2016* discusses the rapid progress made in reaching unreached people groups.

The good news is that there are fewer unreached people groups in the world that have never heard the gospel. The bad news is that we are nonetheless losing ground in world missions. According to OW, "unevangelized populations are multiplying faster than they are being reached for the Gospel."[15]

This should cause us great pause. Despite the billions of dollars and lives poured into world missions over the past decades, we are losing ground in reaching the world for Christ. We believe that we may be getting further behind because most of our efforts, resources, talents, and funds are invested ineffectively, sending

---

[14] Haaries, Jim. The Effectiveness of Short-Term Mission to Africa. Presented at US Centre for World Missions on March 16, 2007.

[15] Operation World's "State of the World Plenary 2016"

Americans rather than equipping nationals. A few Americans are going to get much less of the task done than the many national Christians already in the countries we seek to reach. We could support more available nationals ready to reach their own people for Christ much more effectively.

We realized that if we really wanted to reach the world for Christ, then we needed to get serious about finding better ways to do it, rather than complacently doing whatever seemed best to us at any one moment in time.

Even long-term American missionaries question the impact of short-term missions. In "A Life Overseas," Sarita Hartz discusses "The Mess of Short Term Missions" and "What to Do About Short Term Missions."[16] She writes, "You will not be able to able to impact those [foreign] *beneficiaries* on a day to day, but you can impact the [American] *missionary* who you will get to. That means you probably don't need a team of fifteen people, but rather a smaller, more intentional team." Being involved in long-term overseas mission work as an American herself, her discussion appears to indicate that much of short-term missionary's benefit is to strengthen the American missionaries, rather than to help reach the country and people they are visiting. So, if we did not send Americans on (less effective) long-term missions, there would be even less reason for funding short-term trips. Most of these funds could more effectively be used to fund national Christians.

Sarita Hart also discusses whether there are any sustainable benefits after a short termer goes home. This ties in with "Helping Without Hurting in Short Term Missions," which recommends sending only a few people on a short-term, exploratory team, with the defined objective of finding out how they can effectively assist the local national work on a longer basis, such as by providing financial support for worthy projects. This would enable them to provide a sustainable benefit, and we believe it is a good opportunity and reason for a short-term mission's trip.

---

[16] www.saritahartz.com

Sarita Hart also says, as others do, that part of the benefit of short-term trips is then some short-term westerners may later go to the mission field for a longer term. As a donor or participant, this again can seriously reduce the impact of a gift and might be considered a negative rather than a positive. Since a national could do the work for much less and maybe better, knowing the culture and language, then anything that would redirect funds toward western missionaries and away from indigenous missions could be seen as having a negative impact on our ability to effectively entrust and empower the local church and reach our world for Christ.

We have also heard complaints by the nationals of the time and costs required to host short-term trips by Americans. Anyone who has hosted out of town company before knows the tremendous amount of time, energy, and resources it takes to house, feed, and direct the schedule of visitors. It takes time away from our day-to-day work and activities. Perhaps the desired benefit for host missionaries would come if the guests did in fact decide to make a gift to offset all of the cost it took to host them, plus provide some additional funding for the local work.

Sarita Hart discusses how as a western long-term missionary, she may be more interested in putting the effort out to take care of short-term American missionaries mainly because she was looking for funding help. One wonders why the short-term missionaries wouldn't use the funds raised for their trip to equip and power the ongoing local work?

If fellowship is in fact the real result, we must find more effective ways for a few people to plan a trip to visit friends on a mission field.

One indigenous mission organization we support only recommends one short-term trip and will not receive another without a good reason.

I have not heard many mission organizations discourage short-term trips, perhaps because they do not want to discourage their supporters and possible new supporters. Usually, when I tell the nationals what the trips cost, they wish the money had been sent instead to meet pressing needs in the ongoing work. I think most national organizations hope the Americans will support the ongoing work after their visit, but I have not observed this occurring on a very regular basis.

I do not think most people who go on a short-term trip realize how the cost for their trip could have benefitted the national group short and long-term. I was told recently by a leader of a western group that the national leader was very up front, saying that they did not want many to come, fewer were better, and then only to fit in with what the nationals needed for their ongoing ministry.

As far as support for an American to teach overseas short or long term, I prefer to support the national who may have an advanced degree in theology from a trusted indigenous seminary or Bible College (many do exist, all around the world), knows the language and culture, and costs much less plus hopefully will have experience personally in planting new churches and discipling new believers.

One large missionary-sending organization features an American in a monthly publication who is now serving in his **third** country.[17] It takes years to learn the language and culture. Most new missionaries will not spend the time to learn the language before going and then may return before learning it.

We also know of a young couple who spent years and many thousands of dollars in support preparing to go to the mission field, only to return within six months. After a year or two in the states, they plan to make another go at it next year. What if all of those efforts, time, and funds had instead been sent to equip nationals, with only small, short-term investigatory trips and careful cross-checking? They could have seen great inroads and many souls reached for Christ by now.

One mission organization worked in a country for many years. Their work included building churches. They did not realize this was an American-centric rather than a national-centric model,

---

[17] "Cultivating Nomadic Lives" Commission. Winter 2000. SBC.

until the nationals called to tell them that "your American" church needed painting. When we equip nationals, they can reach their country in ways that are culturally aware and effective in the milieu of their own unique country. Then the local church becomes part and parcel of the local community, instead of being viewed as an unnecessarily foreign and likely unfamiliar implant into the local community.

In Majority World Sending in Perspectives, authors in different areas of the world discuss how they are now sending their people to other countries to engage in missionary work. While Christianity was once largely found in the west and the northern hemisphere, today 78 percent of Christians are from Africa, Asia, and Latin America! Our view of missions as a western-sending effort must change.[18]

Today, country A is sending missionaries to B, B to C, and C to A. Especially with regard to sending long-term missionaries, I have not found a biblical example. The Bible gives many examples of short-term trips by two or three people to entrust the gospel to local faithful leaders, followed by occasional short-term follow-up trips. If a missionary stayed in a place for any longer, it was to train and equip local leaders to whom the new church was then to be entrusted. In addition to questioning our western-centric mindset, this raises the question of whether we are being wise stewards of our resources given high traveling and moving costs, plus the massive time and costs required to learn a new language and culture.

One of the most important lessons we learned from others was one from my own parents. It was to seek to be generous givers. My wife and I followed their example and tithed even during poor times in our life. Later, our giving was increased to over 50 percent. We started giving additional assets as we learned from other Christian businessmen.

Jerry Wear gives examples in his book of fourteen families who have taken a pledge similar to the one promoted by Bill Gates and

---

[18] Operation World's State of the World Plenary 2016.

Warren Buffet in the secular world and have pledged to donating the majority of their wealth.[19]

We have found that what we learned from others often validated what we have seen on mission fields.

Take These Essential Steps...

1. Read Bob Findley's book, "The Future of Foreign Missions."
2. Read "Lessons from the Sapling" by Kurt Alan Ver Beek.
3. Read "Helping Without Hurting in Short-Term Missions."

Record the insights you receive from reading these books. What helped you most?

---

[19] Wear, Jerry. "Kingdom Giving a New perspective on Wealth." 2010. Florida. The Great Commission Foundation of Campus Crusade for Christ.

Chapter 4

Learning from Our Own
Short-Term Trips

*T*hroughout my life, I've taken many short-term international trips, both for consulting, business, missions, and leisure. Through those trips, I have learned some valuable lessons for missions.

Consulting Trips

Early on, one of my experienced mentors told me something I have always remembered. It was that I should not expect to do much good on a short-term assignment. So, the first question was always whether I was doing something for the nationals that they could do for themselves, and then whether there was a better use of the time and money to effectively reach the objective and equip the local people in their agricultural endeavors.

Trips to Brazil, Yugoslavia, and Saudi Arabia were to bring new knowledge of our more advanced irrigation equipment and practices that the local people did not yet have themselves. On a trip to Egypt for the US government, I inspected how Egypt had spent the dollars we had sent for irrigation improvements. On one trip to Libya, I inspected the performance of the US irrigation equipment they had purchased and another trip to evaluate the management of an irrigation project.

All of these trips fit my criteria of going to help the nationals do what they could not (yet) do for themselves. I also learned something about contextualization, or the importance of adjusting what is said based on local conditions. In Egypt, the civil engineer who went with me wanted to judge their bridges over canals based on US standards. I judged them based on whether I thought they were built to have a reasonable life.

In the US forty years ago, center pivot irrigation was coming on very strong. It required little labor but many dollars. I did not promote center pivots for the Yugoslavians, though. They had low cost labor, but not many dollars to purchase the equipment. To be effective, we needed to be sensitive to the unique context in which our ideas would be applied.

My brother gives an example of lack of contextual understanding in one country where he did agronomic evaluations of the soils and concluded a problem was caused by lack of some micro-nutrients. Another person, without analyzing and realizing he was in a country with unusual and unique soil conditions, immediately recommended irrigation. Pride and lack of awareness of the local environment can and often does go before a downfall.

Short-Term Trips to Evaluate Missions and Provide Our Expertise

We have also taken many short-term missions trips in our lives. Some were well justified and effective, and others less so. Here are some brief descriptions of our experiences and what we believe we learned from each. We hope that as we share our experiences, others can build on our successes and avoid our mistakes.

Our first trips were to Mexico to support a Bible College. Later, we extended a modified US Jesus Film program to northwestern Mexico. About 100,000 DVDs were given to churches. It was kept to one DVD per family, so they shared with their family, relations, friends, and business acquaintances. We hired three nationals for two and a half years to equip over 1,000 churches. The Jesus Films were also used in prisons and on buses.

As stewards of what God had given us, we received reports and visited approximately every quarter to review results. We saw church growth from the work. Later, we continued support for the key indigenous leader because he was instrumental in continuing to lead Tijuana in city-wide evangelism. We believe these were a good use of funds, working with local leadership, evaluating results, and visiting periodically to review the work.

We went to the Mideast on a trip to evaluate results of our funding there. We quickly learned that each area and sometimes each country required different programs. Later, we gave to a group working in the area to spread the gospel and disciple. They studied national groups to equip them and provide them with funds. We later applied some of their concepts when we began to focus on a country in southeast Asia.

It does not take much world knowledge to see that many countries do not accept American missionaries. However, with today's technology, there are many effective ways to share the gospel with the people in these countries who are hungry for good news. The key is to find ways not only to evangelize, but also to disciple and help new believers mature in their faith, and then share the good news with others.

American missionaries' work is hampered in countries where foreign Christian missions work is illegal. National Christians could do the work full-time for much less money. There are also other ways of reaching some of these countries for Christ, including using mass media.

We learned an interesting reason why some Americans continued to serve long term as missionaries. One Mideast leader said it was easier for an American to raise $70,000, than for someone from their area to raise the $10,000 needed for a national to support themselves. If this is true, it is extremely unfortunate given the multiplied effectiveness of national missionaries. What can be done to change this misapplication of resources?

Over time, we have come to the conclusion that if we want to reach our world for Christ, then we must begin to think differently about the local church around the world. We must also consider what is an effective use of our time, talents, and resources to support missions work. We believe that the time spent by most Americans going and most funds used to support them would be better spent building relationships with the local church around the world, determining how best to assist the trustworthy among them, and equipping and empowering them.

We were part of a program to train teachers in Russia after Communism fell. We brought and trained them with material they could then use, including the Jesus Film, apologetics, and other biblical material. There was a vacuum in belief that the Russians wanted to fill, so we were bringing knowledge that was not available from the nationals and a program that benefited from American assistance. We believe it was a good use of time and resources. To be eligible to go, we were required to have teaching or management experience.

About twenty-five years ago, we went to a southeast Asian country on a Jesus Film project. The films were not getting coated, thereby reducing their life and usefulness to the indigenous ministry teams. The local director was looking for a US business person to help solve their problems. We visited two local film manufacturers and negotiated with one to buy the equipment to do this. We also saw the need for a generator. They had to completely restart duplication after each power failure, which was happening often. We gave them the funds for the generator, something we would not have known was needed had we not visited their operations. So, we shared our business knowledge in a way that was helpful to their work, including the negotiating skills I had learned from my dad on a small farm in Iowa!

We also observed local Christian leaders who did not need much of our help. They could do evangelism, discipleship, and training, and they knew the languages and the culture.

As we started focusing on a largely unreached southeast Asian country to support church planting work about six years ago, we took another trip to evaluate over twelve indigenous mission groups we had supported or were considering supporting. Since it is very difficult to effectively evaluate local ministries even over many trips, we hired someone to do this for four years. In addition to this, we continued our own studies through other donors, knowledgeable consultants and our readings. We are now able to share the knowledge we gained about trusted local missionaries with others who wish to reach the country for Christ.

Another interesting trip was taken to an Eastern European country to visit a student who had stayed with us years earlier. A Christian conference was occurring, and we were invited to attend. It was a mission organization that mainly served through nationals. However, I was surprised at the number of Americans in the group. One of their American leaders had told me earlier that when they started a new country ministry, if the American was given a one-way ticket, you would usually see more Americans coming to stay. With a two-way ticket, the ministry was more quickly built by effectively training and equipping trustworthy nationals.

As in business, I have seen that taking the easier way out or the path of least resistance often is not the best way.

We passed up on one trip my wife still believes we should have taken. As our business improved twenty-five years ago, we were able to give $25,000 for a Jesus Film translation for Russia. We were invited to the premier showing. Our desire was to go, however, we concluded that the $5,000 in travel expenses could be much better used for additional missions giving. I recall that at that time, we had only started to learn how to evaluate giving results.

We also went to Cuba with hundreds of other Christians. The communist government was concerned and cut off local contacts. I did not see that we did much good except bringing in medical supplies. However, it did give me a US government-approved visit.

I went to Haiti to help a Haitian leader with Partners Worldwide who is successfully helping local businesses to create jobs. American business people go oversees on short term trips as advisors, seeking to equip and empower the local Haitian businessmen, rather than to flood their market with supplies. In contrast, some of the harmful effects of ill-advised foreign assistance to Haiti are explored in the film "Poverty Inc." As locals who have been put out of business by well-meaning supplies, donations, and free construction labor have been known to say, "Who can compete with free?"

I also came across Americans who had gone on short-term trips and later went full time. Apparently, they did not see what I saw. Their cost could have been better used to support a national Christian worker and their presence may have in some regards been harmful to the local economy. When I asked them about their costs and effectiveness compared to a national worker, their justification usually was, "The Lord called me." As with much sending of Americans overseas, it would also be prudent to consider how wise principles and good stewardship enter into the decision of being called?

In traveling to other countries and studying their foreign mission groups, we saw that they mostly did not need us, but sometimes our expertise and a few dollars greatly benefited their outreach. As Dr. Bill Bright, the founder of one of the largest mission groups in the world has stated, "Most of our leaders worldwide are nationals, people born and reared in the country in which they now minister." We believe this is a wise practice. Earlier on in our giving to equip nationals, I was told the story of a Christian hospital in Africa. It had operated for many years, but resulted in few if any new believers. Then, through the efforts of a new church planter coming to the area, many new believers resulted.

On a recent trip to Asia, I observed that it was easy for the national groups to divert funds from church planting to mainly taking care of the many physical needs of the people. The Bible speaks often of helping those in need. However, it also speaks of the horrible end of those without Christ. So, this challenge could be looked at from an opportunity costs viewpoint. How does one provide the most physical benefits to suffering people with the greatest potential of making new disciples?

Steve Saint, in his book "The Great Omission,"[20] tells of American personnel providing medical help to a long line of nationals. Then they needed to return to the US and left a long line of expectant patients wondering why they had not been taken care

---

[20] Saint, Steve. *The Great Omission*. YWAM Publishing (2001)

of. He then came up with a simple dental drill that the nationals quickly learned to operate themselves.

On my trip to Haiti a few years back, I heard of national medical workers who could not compete with all the free help given to Haitians who could afford to pay for services. The medical people had then gone to other places, so they could earn a living. I also met an American medical person who was helping Haiti medical personnel to improve what the nationals did to help those who could not pay.

What if American medical workers helped national workers to provide needed help and medicines that was sustainable after they left? There are examples of simple medical help taught to national churches to provide this on a long-term basis. This can also result in making many more disciples than for American short and long-term trips.

Another example of a church group mostly spending money for travel rather than for long-term benefits to the national group being visited occurred several years back. We were at a fund-raising function for audio Bibles. A church presented their overseas trip whereby they had brought $3000 worth of audio Bibles in the native language but spent $17,000 on the trip. I thought of how much more long-term benefit could have occurred if $17,000 had been spent for audio Bibles and $3000 for the short-term trip.

We also found the worldwide Christians in foreign countries far out-numbered the few American missionaries there. There were already many Christians in most countries that we were sending missionaries to, and we question whether the high-cost foreign western missionaries were really needed there.

I believe that there is some need for short-term mission trips by those with expertise to go on site and evaluate the effectiveness of a program supported, or to evaluate the impact of a gift. We spend less than 5 percent of our giving to evaluate the outcomes of our giving, in addition to funding occasional studies to check out organizations we support, check references with other donors, and sometimes with other national Christians.

Some of my travels to forty countries were really vacations taken for adventure. I see many so-called "missions" trips may unfortunately fall in the category of Christian tourism. None would disagree that long-term foreign missionaries were needed in an earlier time. However, as the demographics of our world continue to change and more effective ways to reach the world arise, my hope is that someday the American church's missions support will shift to effective partnerships with nationals.

On our trips, we soon learned that we were partially welcomed because we had a dollar sign on us. As we were often meeting very poor people, some may have been looking for whatever help they could get from us. They knew of American wealth. One wonders if some raised hands are a disguised request for financial assistance rather than sincere faith? Unless the organizations we visit remain in place and have effective methods of long-term discipleship, there is no way to answer to this question. Steve Corbett and Brian Fikkert also bring this out in "When Helping Hurts."[21]

---

[21] Corbett, Steve & Fikkert, Brian. *When Helping Hurts.* 2009. Illinois. Moody Press.

An American on an overseas mission trip needs to remember that nationals usually see a dollar sign and pay more attention because of the possibility of getting American dollars. (Taken from "When Helping Hurts" by Steve Corbett & Brian Fikkert).

Take These Essential Steps...

Evaluate any past short-term mission trips you or your church have done and determine how successful they were based on what you read in this chapter.

- Were you doing what nationals could have done?
- From an opportunity costs viewpoint, how could you have provided the most physical benefits to suffering people with the greatest potential of making new disciples?
- Did you consider how the costs of the trip could have helped the nationals' ministry you believed in?
- Will you do future short-term trips? If so, how will you maximize their Kingdom effectiveness?

Chapter 5

So Now You Are Interested?

If one agrees with the proposition that the paradigm has changed in missions, how does one start to change their donations and mission trips to be more effective?

Let's review the guidelines from Chapter One:

1. **Determine the goal or objective to achieve in giving.**
2. **Identify the various options or opportunities that could be used to achieve the goal or objective.**
3. **Estimate the cost and potential returns from the main options available. This requires evaluation and study.**
4. **Based on principles of wise stewardship, support the selected mission group.**
5. **Follow up to try to determine what results were obtained and make adjustments as needed.**

The process is then repeated, and new options may be included to consider. Usually for best results, long-term investments, follow-up inspections, and continued knowledge acquisition are required.

We begin by deciding on the goal or goals we seek to achieve with our support, resources, and time. After studying this for some years, we used Paul's example of supporting the preaching of the gospel where it has not been preached (Romans 15:20-21). We picked one southeast Asian country to focus on since it has many unengaged, unreached people groups and unreached people.

We then looked at the options for reaching the country. We had supported the production of gospel tools for many years. However, since our goals also included making disciples, the planting of self-multiplying churches would best fit our goals.

As discussed above, we studied and compared the cost of support for westerners and their relative effectiveness and determined that supporting national organizations was the wisest stewardship choice.

We were then introduced to distance learning for church planting leadership development. They introduced us to various national-run church planting groups. Before investing large sums of money in any of them, we first joined with others to commission a study of these and others we had been introduced to. Besides traveling again to observe the work of these organizations, we hired someone for four years to take five-week trips twice a year to study various church-planting organizations. We also got input from others with knowledge, both within and without the country. We sought to keep these oversight costs down to a small percentage of the total given to mission's work.

As a business person or farmer, the question of Return On Investment and the results or harvest received for a particular investment are important to me. As with opportunity costs, one can invest in a mission opportunity now or later after looking for a return, or results expected through the support given. Investing in a solid indigenous church planting mission, the possibility is to see the number of self-sustaining churches and disciples increase by 20 percent a year.

So, we made the choice between available options. We then took the next step of donating by making some donations to indigenous church planting organizations.

We compared the possible results of these to new ones to whom we had been introduced. Besides the study we had commissioned, we continued to gather more information from other donors involved in the country. The person who was taking trips each year was studying the impact of the ones we supported as well as those we considered supporting.

Based on the evidence gathered, we subtracted a few, added a few, and increased or decreased giving to the others. We continue this process today. We give the most to two organizations and some to others.

Based on the evidence we have, the cost for baptisms or making new disciples for a small part of a US church's budget would equal the US church's yearly baptisms or new disciples. What this also means is that if a small church spent its mission budget on national church planters, they could likely see more believers come into the kingdom through their giving then a mega church's outcome in mission effectiveness. We find great joy seeing God blessing the work we support by His grace and provision. It is our hope and prayer that other churches will begin to re-focus their efforts, and that we can see millions and billions more unreached people who are able to hear the gospel and trust in Christ through the work of these churches.

As we examine outcomes from the missions work we support, we also look at longer term church attendance and try to factor in attrition of new churches and membership. We support training, tools, and entrance strategies to an unreached people group, and sometimes pastoral support to a new unreached people group. We also try to budget our giving to support church planting activities longer term.

By God's grace, our business can provide reasonable levels of support to various organizations year after year. Some of this may not apply to other mission supporters. Rather than support six plus organizations like we do, an individual might only support a couple of organizations, or they may be able to support many more than we do.

I was once accused of possibly being an instrument to help save many people, yet not help them improve their physical wellbeing. We do support organizations whose work brings about physical healing as well as family and community transformation as they bring the gospel of salvation. Another part of the answer to this is once the people we are reaching become Christians, they have hope that they did not have before. This may also be the reason so many of them are coming to Christ. Their nation's religion devalues them and puts them at the bottom of society.

As they come to Christ and their lives change, they quit drinking and gambling which improves the family's life. The churches are also encouraged to take care of the orphans and widows. Church planting organizations also promote better hygiene and occupational training.

The Bible has many exhortations to take care of the poor. We have been introduced to literacy training of illiterate adults, particularly women. The cost of one short term American trip would take care of fifty to one hundred students for a year of night school for reading, writing, math, hygiene, and occupational skill. This changes a family and the children in many profound, life-changing ways.

Being taught by Christians, many become Christians. So, besides filling a social need, it fills a spiritual need. To us, the question is always, "Are we promoting a social, work-based gospel or a Christ-centered gospel?"

We believe this program brings the beautiful kingdom of God in all its aspects to unreached areas in Christ's name.

So, we have gone full circle from establishing a goal(s), to options, to evaluating options, to donating, to inspecting impact, and back to a goal(s). We continue this cycle but do not try to change our giving much year to year to an organization, especially if our donations are over 10 percent of an organization's funding, or they may have difficulty retaining national programs and staff.

Impact

I have utilized Americans and nationals to vet an organization's impact toward our goals. There have been questions raised about the American who went over twice a year, and whether mission visits were sufficient to do an adequate job. Yet, he had much more experience with various mission works than most short termers and even some long term American missionaries. Another foundation funding indigenous church planters much prefers information from knowledgeable local Christians for vetting. The original model from one region of the world, on which we based our own model, used deep vetting before giving by employing Americans with much overseas experience in the area.

The question arises, how much of an organization's funds go to support the mission and how much is used for administration and fund raising? The percentage for raising funds and vetting overseas-national mission work is usually higher than for US missions. However, the overall costs of ministry are significantly lower, and the results are much better. We prefer that nearly all the overseas costs are for the nationals and not for Americans going overseas long-term to do and/or oversee the work. Some might call the latter a colonial mission.

In the past, we have given to a cause where the administrative and fundraising costs were borne by others and 100 percent of donors' funds went into overseas programs. However, the program costs went to sending Americans overseas long term. We did not support this. I later learned the program we did support was not in their field of expertise which we then stopped supporting. We continue to support an organization which provides administrative and fundraising costs from a small group of donors, enabling others' gifts to entirely support the work of indigenous Christians.

We see that by partnering with the existing church in the country, local Christians are trained and equipped, and much is accomplished for a relatively small investment.

The biggest benefit is to raise funds to equip national Christians who know the language and culture and spend only a small percent for vision trips and inspection of what is expected.

I have visited with the mission pastors of several large churches. My goal has been to show them the much greater impact their church could have if the mission money went to equip and support nationals rather than to send Americans. I quickly learned that their main emphasis in giving was to support mostly members from their congregation who believed they were called to go to a foreign country to bring the gospel. We had observed this when we were on a mission's committee some years before. At the time, we did not think much of it since we had not been introduced to the greater impact of supporting nationals.

While discussing my thoughts on equipping nationals rather than sending Americans, the mission chairman of a large church immediately told me about a bad experience they had supporting one indigenous missionary who had just taken their money for other purposes than spreading the gospel. I reminded him of an American they had also sent overseas, at a multiplied greater cost than the national, and who had mostly failed in his mission. I also wondered how the church could do their due diligence in evaluation while supporting a small amount of many Americans in so many countries. I wondered why they didn't focus on only a few to do a better job of monitoring their giving and maintaining a higher level of accountability.

It is also interesting that many churches will claim an American missionary because they give maybe 5 to 10 percent of the missionary's support. I think this and sending to many countries may give them the sense that they are better following the command to go into all the world and preach the gospel. If this church wanted to do this, their mission budget could have fully supported two national pastors in many different countries.

The other aspect that surprised me was that their previous emphasis on the 10/40 window, where many have never even heard the gospel, no longer seemed to apply in their sending.

In summary, it took us many years to become centered on making disciples and getting the most disciples for the dollar expended. I have found most, if not all, churches count new baptisms each year but give most of their mission money to send Americans, short or long term, resulting in many fewer new disciples overall than if the principles promoted in this book were followed. Most also do little to reach international students and immigrants in the US. We have found in the distribution of Jesus DVDs to students and immigrants that some would end up being sent or used back in their home country. Once they become Christians they also bring the gospel back to their home country in other ways.

Chapter 6

Sustainability/Dependency

*I*n one of my discussions with a church leader, I asked
him why his church and denomination only supported
Americans overseas and not the nationals whom we put most of
our giving. A big reason seemed to be that my way may not be sustainable if money was no longer allowed into the country for their
support. I know that in the country we were discussing, Americans
probably were not even allowed to work with the nationals.

In addition, a study comparing American and indigenous missionaries shows that the only missionaries who receive any support
from the country in which they serve are indigenous missionaries.
The American mission groups were wholly dependent on U.S. support. If one's goal is sustainability, the indigenous workers seem to
be a much better choice. I wondered about this man's conclusions
about dependency.

In a report not allowed for publication, on the growth or
maybe mostly stagnation of the Pakistani church, some interesting points came out on this subject. Many of the earlier foreign missionaries had left. The funding for their projects was also
vastly reduced. In many cases, like the western missionaries we have
studied, these western missionaries also had not trained leaders

to take their place. So much of the past effort of the donors and foreign missionaries did not proceed and seemed to be stagnating.

The question essentially boils down to: what would be sustainable if funds/personnel/resources were no longer allowed to be sent? When looked at in this way, we believe our own national Christian-equipping model is much more sustainable than the American-sending model ever can be.

For example, without materials the literacy training could end without funds going into a country. However, the benefits of the training would remain, and those who had been trained and were discipled in new churches could continue to help and reach others in Christ's name. Because new believers would be able to read God's word for themselves, they could continue to learn and grow in their faith.

Westerners reaching out to UUPGs or UPGs would be hindered if foreign funds were cut off and a relatively immature church would be left to flounder without leadership. However, if training continued by already trained and equipped nationals, church-planting pastors could expand the church to nearby villages causing the church to continue to grow and flourish even if western support stopped.

Often, some entrance strategies such as literacy or children's clubs help pave the way for planting a new church. We have also supported church planting through micro financing, but the cost of one method was $800+ per family in the village. This high cost method would slow down or stop with no new foreign funds. Because of this, "How Helping Hurts" suggests micro finance that starts not with foreign funds, but from the national participants themselves.

In my study of what happened to the spread of the gospel in China after the Americans were expelled, it appears that the growth continued through the efforts of local believers. Although there are still many, many unreached people in China, the local church continues to grow there.

Early training of new converts to give, and hopefully tithe, improves sustainability and reduces dependency. An example of this for a very poor group is the Mizo's Handful of Rice. It is the story of very poor Indian Christians supporting their own church and also mission workers by taking out handfuls of rice from their meager supplies for giving.

I have come across examples of national Asian mission organizations raising funds from middle to high income Asians. One American mission group working in Asia through nationals also raised funds to be used in their country. We believe these are all promising developments.

Chapter 7

Mission Giving: Ten Times Plus Returns

*I*n deciding where to give, one must look at the goals or
results desired. Our goals are to give for evangelism, discipleship, and church planting with some help for physical and
social needs, particularly in areas where the gospel is seldom heard.

*Since there are many groups with American missionaries who have
specific expertise and who take short-term trips overseas,
how does one differentiate between potential donor recipients?*

The following story may best illustrate this. A long-term
American overseas missionary questioned a national mission leader.

"How do you find such strong national leaders when we have
trouble finding any good national leaders?"

The national leader replied, "The short-term American missionary we work with trains us and then goes home."

There are many stories and much evidence that the money
given to send American missionaries overseas was not always very
effective giving. The same is true at times for national missionaries.
Giving to several agencies may be like investing in several stocks
for diversification.

Regarding funding nationals and minimizing dependency, David Garrison of the IMB asks, "What sort of things fit into the category of primary evangelization? Missionaries to unreached people groups, Bible translation and distribution, gospel literature production and distribution, radio broadcasts and other evangelistic media ministries, church planter training centers and material, and new leadership development programs all require external funding to get underway."[22] I agree with satisfying these needs.

We do not give to build churches. These are costly and rapid, solid church planting can occur with house churches. This also happened in China house churches after the American missionaries were kicked out. The nationals sometimes build churches with their own funds. We have supported tools such as the Jesus Film and audio tools such as The Proclaimer. Since many unreached people are illiterate, these tools can be important. Literacy training makes it possible for new believers to read the Word and grow in their faith. However, we do not give advice to the mission organizations we support on these matters. We mainly look for accountability on making disciples and church planting where the results will stick for many years. One possibility to check this is a random audit of results claimed, much as an auditor would do in checking a company's finances. One of the organizations we support has an "auditor" and we also do our own auditing of results.

We are shy of supporting Bible schools for a few years of training. We prefer on-the-job training, which with the right program, can be extremely effective. One reason is because unreached areas normally are not developed and often do not have good sanitary facilities. The schools usually have good facilities, which could discourage a graduate from going to unreached areas where there is poor sanitation and no clean water. We have also heard reports that more of the graduates go into call centers upon graduation than into church planting.

---

[22] Garrison, David. 2004. *Church Planting Movements*. p. 267. WIGTake Resources.

We do not spend much on sending Americans to train, since there are usually huge culture and language barriers which are difficult and costly to overcome. Another reason is that the local trainers with Masters degrees in theology we have supported can work full-time, year-round for the same cost as two short-term trips by Americans. Obviously, a great deal more is accomplished in a year by the two trained indigenous workers we supported than the Americans, who are there in a foreign country for a very short time and who may have no experience planting churches.

After being a high school dropout, but then going on for my Ph.D. in engineering, it would be easy to be prejudiced towards higher education and those who have advanced degrees. I think it does help me in research. However, I looked up to my father who only got an eighth-grade education in the Netherlands. He was a deep student of the Bible, served on many more positions than me in churches, Christian schools, and on college boards. We have never seen a measurable difference in job performance in our farm managers based on their education.

I remember one experience soon after I received my Masters of Science degree in engineering. We were contracted to water fill-dirt in borrow pits and cut areas. A flood had occurred and had washed away seventy thousand cubic yards of dirt that the contractor had to replace. The state did not resurvey it, so I offered to do the resurvey and calculate the number of cubic yards of dirt that had washed away. Part of my pitch was that I had a Masters of Science degree in engineering, including surveying.

The old contractor looked at me and said, "I will not hold that against you."

He may have spit his tobacco on his floorboard, but he was a self-made multi-millionaire and I was not. We both got the job done. I could quickly add numbers in my head while he very slowly did it on paper, but I made a few more mistakes than he did!

Another American pastor training in the Philippines tells a story of a young man in his class. After the first week's training, each one was instructed to go out on the weekend to do evangelism.

On Monday, the class was asked how the weekend went. The young man volunteered that he had started a class with a few interested people.

When asked what he taught he said, "What you taught us the first week!"

This is what he did each week thereafter with the new material he learned.

As with the early church, bringing the gospel message starts with the simple message of God the Father's love for us in Christ by His Spirit. Most believers never get into the deeper material that theologians disagree on. When they do, there are many local seminaries, attended by indigenous leaders who can serve in areas of theological oversight and denominational leadership.

Chapter 8

A Case Study:
My Haiti Short-Term Missions Trip

*W*hile in Florida in February 2011, I flew to Haiti for five days. I went with Partners Worldwide to consult with Haitian businesses to help them grow. With 80 percent unemployment, additional jobs are critical in Haiti.

I hoped some of my experiences would be of help to these struggling entrepreneurs. Daniel, a Haitian with a BS and MBA from the US, was the national running the program. He also has some business experience. It was good to see someone of his caliber and experience go back to his country to help. I provided advice to him and also to some local businesses. He also presented the need for a conference and a small loan to a business, and we provided the requested funds for both because the needs were determined by the indigenous people instead of western resources being dumped willy-nilly without regard to the local economy. I believe the gifts were effective.

One of my purposes for going to Haiti was also to check on the return on investment from Americans on short-term trips providing construction labor in Haiti. Local labor costs in Haiti are $3 to $10 per day, even for skilled labor. Despite the fact that many Haitians were in need of work, I met various American groups there to provide their labor, and to build or rebuild for free. The cost for them to come and stay was usually $1000 for two weeks–yielding maybe ten total days of work.

The $1000 that these American short-term missionaries spent provided on average only $30 to $100 of labor benefits in terms of the local labor rates. It also took away local employment where 80 percent are unemployed. Ver Beek cites one group that spent $30,000 in travel to build one $2,000 house. The long-term impact on Haiti has been as heartbreaking as it was unintended. As Corbett and Fikkert urge us, Christians seeking to help must consider the long-term impacts of our efforts to "help" and to make sure we are not actually hurting the recipients of our assistance.

Or as Steve Saint, in *The Great Omission* puts it, "When in the name of Christian missions, we do for indigenous believers what they can do for themselves, we undermine the very church that God has sent us to plant."

In many developing countries, one could find the same general wage scale and high unemployment. To call short-term missions to these countries an effective missions trip, even with some encouragement and evangelism thrown in, is very questionable. Alternatively, one could provide the money for six to twelve months of employment for a local Christian, who could work and do evangelism far in excess of what an American can do in two weeks. While this does require some initial research and networking to make sure we are entrusting the gospel and our resources to local trustworthy Christians, that time and effort yields rich dividends in the local church and community into the future, instead of crippling the very people we had hoped to assist.

The converse is also true. There are times when the local people are very much in need of resources and knowledge which they lack. In those cases, westerners are welcome and can provide tremendous support and assistance.

While in Haiti, I came across reports that some local medical people had left the country because they could not compete with "free." Now there was an immediate and maybe more of a long-term need for medical help for some very poor people. However, the people who could afford some help were using the free help. Therefore, the Haitian medical personnel could not compete with free. What was intended to help a very poor country wound up further wounding and crippling its people and its economy.

Free food from overseas can also cause great damage to local growers—like other local businesses, they cannot compete with "free." I have read stories of this occurring in Haiti and many other countries.

Perhaps not surprisingly, as Hurricane Matthew hit Haiti in October of 2016, Haitians pled with foreign countries *not* to give to aid organizations such as the American Red Cross. The need was great, but they asked that we instead provide real, lasting help to Haitians through local Haitian aid organizations, lists of which began to be distributed, and also through tourism to Haiti. This was a clear statement of caution by those who were unintentionally devastated by previous assistance from countries such as the U.S.

There are also many examples of effective assistance which has been given. Some U.S. farmers provide free food in needy areas by providing funds to **buy grain from the local farmers** in a country with a famine. The farmers give acres of grain in the US, which is sold to the local US grain elevator. The sale proceeds are sent to the country with the famine to buy the local grain instead of flooding the market with free food, thereby helping local farmers instead of putting them out of business. The Food Resource Bank or FRB takes care of this for the US farmers who wish to help.

I met one woman with an organization that was helping local medical providers to better perform their work. We believe like her that the best help to provide is what will endure after we return home. When our short-term efforts help only a few of the people and cripple those who could provide substantial help for the long-term, we can only imagine the pain we cause.

I also travelled with Daniel Jean-Louis while in Haiti. He wrote "From Aid to Trade," which discusses the failure of the foreign aid models. He put on a conference to attempt to get the NGOs sending free materials into Haiti to buy from the locals instead, so the fragile local businesses were not forced to compete with free.

In many cases, even if it is carefully targeted, the level of medical help available in the US is not always the best solution. It may be better to teach locals basic medical care for a large number than specialized care for a few. In "The Great Omission" by Steve Saint, he discusses a rudimentary manual drill to repair teeth in a jungle setting. The natives only had a few hours training but did very well.

Chapter 9

Why We Support National Workers

*And thus I aspired to preach the gospel, not where Christ was
already named, that I might not build upon another
man's foundation. (Romans 15:20)*

"What we have seen and heard we proclaim to you also,"
(1 John 1:4). This is our journey to give a large percentage of our mission support to equip national missionaries,
rather than sending Americans.

In the past forty-five years of travel to many overseas countries
for consulting, missions, adventure, and our study of where God is
working in foreign missions, we learned many things that we now
apply to our mission giving. Bob *Findley's The Future of Foreign*
Mission has significantly influenced us.

We found that the world had changed in missions. Many
faithful missionaries have brought the gospel to the unreached
world in the last 200 to even 2,000 years, so there are now many
national Christians in relatively unreached countries.

The following figure shows what we have personally observed
and heard described by others, when comparing the American
leadership model with the work of indigenous mission's leaders.

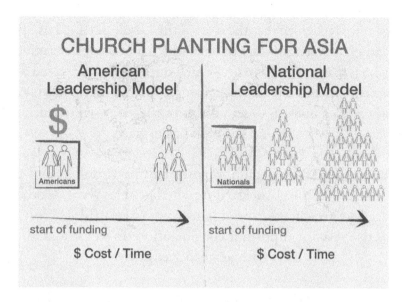

High dollar costs, and significantly lower results, are usually associated with sending Americans.

Our use of ineffective mission's methods is not free of implications. There are still many people in the world who have never heard the name of Jesus. In the meantime, many are going to eternity without the gospel as the image below shows.

Again we recognize that the work is the Lord's and it is His Spirit and His sovereign will, not ours, which ultimately determines who is reached and when. We are nonetheless not excused for poor choices and unwise stewardship. Our love for our Savior and the world compels us to seek the most effective ways to reach the world with His saving grace.

The method is important because of available dollars and the time to get the gospel to unreached people. While God is indeed sovereign, we cannot ignore wise stewardship. Cost and effectiveness are important considerations in world missions as with any other effort.

We believe we are stewards of what God has given us. The problems are not always avoidable. No one and nothing in this world is perfect. We accept some dependency and waste for a low-cost national worker rather than what we consider much greater problems resulting from sending high-priced American missionaries overseas for the long term.

We do not pay for church buildings nor support national workers endlessly. Rather, we provide for national training and equipping to make it possible for them to effectively reach their own country for Christ. We have concluded that the raising of indigenous support in totally unreached areas is not possible until people have been evangelized and at least a few churches are planted where people can grow in their faith. As the local Christian community grows, so too can support for the local church. As long as we do not provide expensive buildings and send expensive workers, the costs of the local church can grow in proportion to the financial abilities of the area. In relatively impoverished areas, churches supported by the local people may look very different from churches in more wealthy areas. This is only possible when one supports local Christians who will use methods best suited to the local area in which they are serving.

Case Study

In conclusion, we do have the following real-life case study comparing the work of an American-led group with indigenous national church planting organizations to the same UUPG.

American led group

Two 2-year Americans at $45,000 per year	$90,000
Eight short term trips per year at $4000 each	32,000
American already in-country at $70,000 per year (assume ½ time for 10 UUPGs, divide by 10 for one UUPG)	3,500
Total	**$125,500**

For two Americans studying the language and culture and 8 short term American trips

National leadership and church-planting efforts

Three indigenous Muslim background believer church planters' support, training and coordination	$6,000
Six church planters' support training and coordination	14,400
Training of 20 church planters in Bild material at $420 each	8,400
Trainer $2500 per year for 1/5th time	500
Higher level trainer with MS in theology plus experience $5000 x 10%	500

National leadership and church-planting efforts

Inspection $300 per Unreached Unengaged People Group by American with national help	300

National leadership and church-planting efforts

Total **$30,100**

For nine national church planters' support, training, and coordination and training for an additional 20 national church planters.

The American led group spent two years and an extra $200,000 just to learn what the national church planting groups already knew.

Presented at Finishing The Task 2012

Final Word

Could I Be Wrong?

Could I be wrong in my growing, strong belief against supporting most American sending short- and long-term mission trips?

This thought should always come to mind when one has a minority or contrarian viewpoint. Though mine is almost an outlier viewpoint, I believe it is supported by thirty years of study, travel, and my experiences equipping nationals rather than sending Americans, donating, and inspecting results along with many other Americans doing the same thing.

I have concluded that the changing viewpoint on slavery among Christians over the years is helpful. Unfortunately, some of the largest U.S. denominations initially did not agree with northern Christians that slavery was evil. It took them years to repent and turn from their earlier views. In England, Wilberforce could not for many years convince the legislators to outlaw slave trade. Today, with the benefit of hindsight, we would likely agree that the southern view and the English legislation supporting slavery were tragically, horribly wrong.

Today, in many churches and denominations, short- and long-term sending of Americans is still strongly encouraged by the churches and denominations. In my studies, I cannot find much research on stewardship in sending Americans. The studies we have personally commissioned certainly do not support the practice, nor does there seem to be a scriptural command to send westerners rather than entrusting the gospel to trustworthy Christians in the area who can be trained and equipped to teach others. With the billions of dollars spent on missions and the apparent lack of evidence for this viewpoint, I am hopeful that Christian colleges will carry forward our research on this important issue.

After careful analysis, I continue to believe that our position is well-founded, despite the fact that it is not widely accepted in many churches today.

First, I believe that this information has not been widely disseminated. Many people continue to send Americans on short- and longer-term mission trips simply because they are not aware that there is another way or do not know the reasons for supporting indigenous Christians. They are not aware that there are ways to become familiar with, support, and receive accountability from indigenous Christian missionaries, or of the huge differences in costs and results. They do not realize that current methods are losing ground in world missions. I am hopeful that this book will join with other voices to help raise awareness on this important issue.

Second, I have found there are many faithful, trustworthy Christians in most countries that Americans go to as missionaries, that with a little effort and assistance from knowledgeable people, could perform very well the position that the American would do, assuming part of the American's cost was used to cover the national's cost.

In the movie "The Case for Christ," Lee Strobel, as an attorney, refers to hard evidence to support or take away the claim of Christ's resurrection. I have tried to use my training and experience to evaluate "The Case for Stewardship" in mission support and evaluating whether to send Americans on short- or long-term mission trips versus equipping nationals to finish the task.

I am particularly surprised when I read advice to individuals and churches to send inexperienced Americans to figure out how to reach an unreached people group. This could be considered the same as using amateurs, made exponentially worse by the fact that they often don't even understand the language or the culture.

A side-by-side comparison of this method with the outcomes of supporting national missionaries is shown in the chapter, "Why We Support Nationals." The pastor in this example justified the $200,000 extra cost and two years just to **learn about** an unreached people group which the **nationals were already reaching** and who could have greatly increased their reach with a few more dollars in support.

Some may say that they are more comfortable trusting relatively ineffective foreign Americans who are known, rather than national missionaries who they do not (yet) know. We would agree that egregious examples of waste can be found both among national workers as well as among Americans who have been sent. It is essential to establish accountability and follow-up in either case. However, it is much easier to establish accountability with a national working with an indigenous missions group than over a lone American with no one nearby to answer to.

In addition, there is a much greater margin of error because of the massive cost of sending an American. Just one undetected western missionary gone astray can set a mission effort back by hundreds of thousands or even a million dollars and decades of time. We personally know of at least one such American missionary. By comparison, one national missionary gone awry will set the missions work back by much less.

In addition, a study comparing American church planting organizations with indigenous efforts shows that the local indigenous church is much more willing to be accountable and to report detailed outcomes and information to supporters than are American organizations.[23] This is true despite the fact that the

---

[23] See Missionary Cost Effectiveness Summary in Appendix 1.

indigenous missionaries face perhaps an even greater risk of persecution for their missionary activity in their own country.

We support national pastors who already live in the country and are planting churches for as little as $2,000 a year. Two trainers with Masters degrees in theology get $5,000 and $6,000 a year. We supported someone in the Mideast for $10,000 a year and when looking at supporting a pastor in Eastern Europe, the cost was approximately the same. Most reports show Americans overseas cost $60,000 to $70,000 a year.

Often it is difficult to really know how God is working in an area, since raised hands are often equated with making disciples. We recognize that the Holy Spirit works to soften hearts, and that this is not man's work. Moreover, God is sovereign, and His purposes will not fail. However, we don't believe that any of this relieves us of our responsibility to God to seek to reach the lost and to be wise stewards of the resources He has given. We seek to be faithful, recognize the work to be wholly His, and pray and trust that He will bless mission's efforts. I have talked to many short-term mission returnees and asked what results they saw. Some claim many raised hands but showed little tie-in to making disciples.

In talking with Americans who agree that a national Christian could do what they did for much less, there seems to be no indication that stewardship of God's assets used to support them was ever considered.

Working through local mission organizations in one country, I have come across many American Christians short- and long-term, even though there are over 20,000,000 Christians in this country today. Many of these millions would become full-time Christian workers if support and training were provided. We do not hesitate to support a pastor for church planting in the U.S., but paradoxically consider it establishing "dependency" over there. To the contrary, the only missionaries in this country who report receiving support from local Christians are the indigenous missionaries, those from the country itself. Apparently, the American missionaries are in much greater danger of dependency and are much less sustainable than indigenous missionaries.

After studying the local Christian population and potential evangelists and trainers, I have not come across any countries where I saw the need to send Americans rather than supporting nationals. When we did support work in those countries, it was also through satellite, social media, and other means.

I have come across a few American missionaries whom I would call outliers that are very gifted. However, I have also found many national Christian leaders who I would consider outliers and are very gifted. I have come across some Americans who go in small groups for short-term trips to provide training and teaching to indigenous Christians, which was probably needed. These may be well justified short-term trips, and they do not mark Christianity as a foreign religion like a larger, longer-term group of Americans quickly would.

However, there appear to be a number of short-term teachers who are attempting to impart to others what their own churches in the U.S. do not exhibit. The ability of a U.S. leader, whose own church is not growing, evangelizing, or birthing new churches is questionable. The problem is exacerbated by their lack of knowledge about the language and culture.

This reminds me of the time a church we attended was promoting the Kennedy evangelism method. The pastor and three of us showed up. He gave us some instruction and then sent us forth in the neighborhood to knock on doors and present something on the gospel. My wife and another woman paired up and I was by myself. I could really have benefitted from his accompanying me and guiding me.

There is a slow shift in recognizing that the work of evangelism and discipleship in foreign countries can be done more effectively, faster, and at a much lower cost by nationals, but change is very slow. The verse, "Going into all the world and preach the gospel" is often used to send Americans. The most important part is "make disciples" which short-term trips usually do not end up accomplishing. I fear the verse may be misinterpreted, with tragic results for world missions. How does one person or a church go into "all" the world? And how does this apply to my mother, who in her later years was unable to leave her room yet continued to support missions work? Are mission supporters such as her not considered among those who are faithfully making disciples?

I am not a Bible scholar, but I am told Mark 16:15 can also be translated, "So wherever you go in the world, tell everyone the Good News" (NOG).[24]

Even millions of dollars from an individual or church may be better used to equip nationals in only one country to improve the inspection of what is expected. We believe that as we equip and train indigenous missionaries, we are "sending" them to reach their own country for Christ, just as surely as if we "sent" someone from our church here in the U.S. We believe wise stewardship and scripture calls us to "send" and entrust the gospel to trustworthy, indigenous Christians rather than continuing to send long- or short-term western missionaries, long after the beautiful local church has been established in a country.

I have donated to and worked with two denominations over the years. Inexplicably, many continue using the old model of spending millions to send Americans, often even not to unreached people groups or the 10/40 Window, where most of the unreached people in our world live.

After recently viewing a Christian organization's presentation of an aspect of one of their evangelism, discipleship, and social programs, my thought was that theirs was a very high-priced and relatively ineffective method of evangelism and discipleship. Someone who observed their social programs in person shared, that from his point of view, the hundreds of millions they raised each year led to high priced social programs with very little Christian impact.

---

[24] Names of God Bible (NOG) The Names of God Bible (without notes) © 2011 by Baker Publishing Group.

If your church spends most of its mission giving to send Americans and you want it to make many more disciples through equipping nationals, share this book with your pastor and mission committee.

You can make a rough calculation of the effectiveness of your church's mission program by dividing the money spent for equipping nationals to the overall mission budget. You could also include the money that is raised from the congregation for short-term mission trips as part of the overall mission budget. A low percentage usually indicates an ineffective mission's program.

- **Determine the goal or objective to achieve in giving.**
- **Identify the various options or opportunities that could be used to achieve the goal or objective.**
- **Estimate the cost and potential returns from the main options available. This requires evaluation and study.**
- **Based on principles of wise stewardship, support the selected mission's group or missionary.**
- **Follow up to try to determine what results were obtained and make adjustments as needed.**

Appendix 1

Missionary Cost Effectiveness Study Summary

by Excellence in Giving 2012

*T*he following are conclusions from a study on American Missionary Cost Effectiveness in an Asia country with eight mission organizations having over 10,000 American foreign missionaries compared to National mission organizations.

1. The most fruitful missionary teams spent the most time training nationals. The lowest cost of any American group was $5,258 per church plant. Unfortunately, American missionaries only spent 18% of their time training nationals.

2. Indigenous ministries are 23 times more cost effective at planting churches than Americans.

3. Each American missionary costs were 40 times national church planter costs. The investment cost for American Missionaries to be linguistically ready and culturally established by the fifth year on the field is $232,368 compared to $4,800 to $6,000 for four years of supporting a national church planter.

4. American missionaries raise an average of $71,000 per year compared to $1,200 to $1,440 for nationals.
5. Since national church planters raise much more of their funds locally, dependency and sustainability is much less of a factor for the national than for American church planters.
6. American missionaries spend a significant amount of time doing tasks that the nationals could do.
7. The majority of American missionaries count church plants with 1-5 people involved, whereas 7 of 8 national groups surveyed require 10 or more for a church.

About the Author

The author is a businessman, entrepreneur, inventor, and national mission donor. He holds a Ph.D. in irrigation engineering from Colorado State University and has worked at the University of Nebraska. He and his wife Betty have three children and eight grandchildren. His hobbies include business, travel, and reading. He can be reached at john.addink@gmail.com.

CPSIA information can be obtained
at www.ICGtesting.com
Printed in the USA
FSHW010243130819